Searchlight BOOKS

High-Tech Science

Explore Forensic Science

Abbe Lynn Starr

Lerner Publications ◆ Minneapolis

Lerner Publications Company
An imprint of Lerner Publishing Group, Inc.
241 First Avenue North
Minneapolis, MN 55401 USA

For reading levels and more information, look up this title at www.lernerbooks.com.

Main body text set in Adrianna Regular.
Typeface provided by Chank.

Editor: Brianna Kaiser **Designer:** Martha Kranes

Library of Congress Cataloging-in-Publication Data

Names: Starr, Abbe L., author.
Title: Explore forensic science / Abbe Lynn Starr.
Description: Minneapolis : Lerner Publications, [2024] | Series: Searchlight books—High-tech science | Includes bibliographical references and index. | Audience: Ages 8–11 | Audience: Grades 4–6 | Summary: "Forensic science helps to determine the cause of somebody's death and to catch people who have committed a crime. Learn about the history of forensics, the latest tools and techniques forensic scientists use, and more"— Provided by publisher.
Identifiers: LCCN 2023006981 (print) | LCCN 2023006982 (ebook) | ISBN 9798765608944 (library binding) | ISBN 9798765617069 (epub)
Subjects: LCSH: Forensic sciences—Juvenile literature. | Crime scene investigations—Juvenile literature. | BISAC: JUVENILE NONFICTION / Law & Crime
Classification: LCC HV8073.8 .S73 2024 (print) | LCC HV8073.8 (ebook) | DDC 363.25—dc23/eng/20230421

LC record available at https://lccn.loc.gov/2023006981
LC ebook record available at https://lccn.loc.gov/2023006982

Manufactured in the United States of America
1-1009441-51572-4/19/2023

Table of Contents

Chapter 1

ALL ABOUT FORENSIC SCIENCE

Are you ready to be a detective? Science is here to help! Forensic science is the use of scientific knowledge to solve a crime. Forensic scientists find evidence that can be used in a court of law. Evidence shows proof that a person is guilty or innocent.

forensic firsts

In 1910 French forensic scientist Edmond Locard opened the first forensic science lab to fight crime. He solved mysteries by studying clues like dust, hair, and threads from clothes and figured out a way to compare fingerprints.

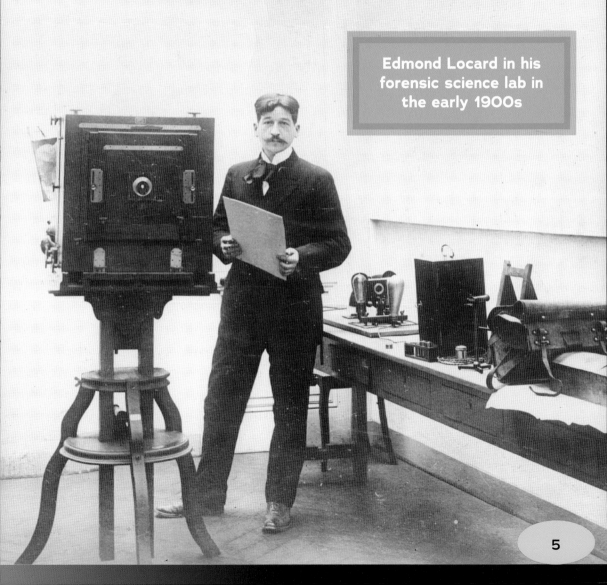

Edmond Locard in his forensic science lab in the early 1900s

People have unique, or one-of-a-kind, fingerprints. Fingerprints have different patterns of arches, whorls, and loops. In the 1920s the US Federal Bureau of Investigation (FBI) created a national pool of fingerprint files. Forensic scientists could read and compare fingerprints from the pool. A computer database of fingerprints replaced this pool in 1999.

Fingerprints have unique patterns.

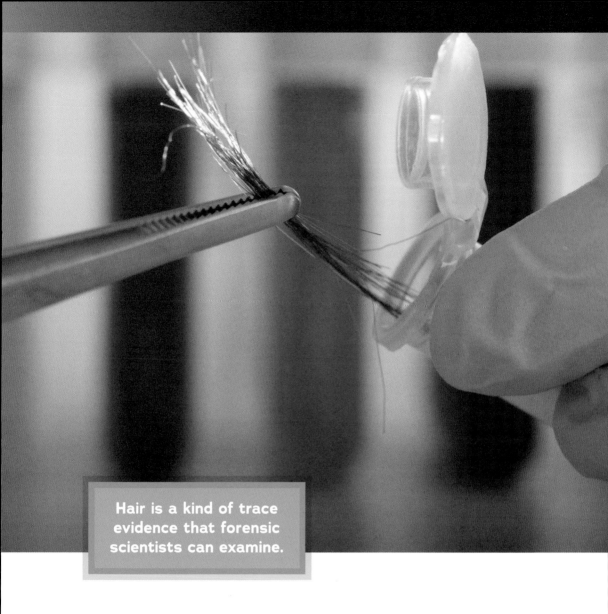

Hair is a kind of trace evidence that forensic scientists can examine.

New discoveries such as unique fingerprints help scientists find people who commit crimes. Some people who commit crimes wear gloves to hide their fingerprints and find ways to not leave trace evidence at the scene. Forensic scientists must continue to research to stay ahead of them.

Science Fact or Science Fiction?

Forensic science began in the 1900s.

That is fiction! An autopsy is the examination of a dead body to figure out the cause of death. The first forensic autopsy was in 44 BCE. Physician Antistius examined Julius Caesar's body after he was stabbed to death. Antistius shared his results in the Roman forum, a location that was important in ancient Rome. The word *forensic* comes from the Latin word *forensis*, meaning "before the forum." Forensic science got its name from this time in history.

Statue of Julius Caesar

Solving Crime

Many sciences like biology, chemistry, physics, engineering, and computer science are needed to solve crimes. When scientists use their knowledge and examine clues, they can find out what happened at a crime scene even if no one saw the crime take place.

SCIENTISTS EXAMINE EVIDENCE FROM CRIME SCENES.

Chapter 2

BODIES, BUGS, AND BONES

Scientists look at many factors at a crime scene such as a person's wounds, broken glass, or strange stains. Each clue helps tell the story of what happened. Sometimes scientists use clever ways to search a crime scene. Dogs, bugs, wounds, and bones all reveal evidence in the most unusual ways.

Dogs can use their sense of smell to help find evidence.

Dogs and Smell

Dogs make great detectives. Did you know that a dog's sense of smell is about 10,000 times stronger than a human's? Some dogs, usually Labradors or German shepherds, are trained to learn the smell of decomposition—something that is rotting.

When bodies decompose, a chemical reaction takes place. This reaction produces a very strong smell. Living people have unique smells, but dead bodies smell alike.

A SCIENTIST LOOKING AT EVIDENCE UNDER A MICROSCOPE

▼

A dog will sniff out this smell. Once it finds the smell, the dog sits or lies down and barks. This lets the police know where a body is.

After a body is found, forensic scientists do an autopsy. Forensic scientists look for evidence inside and outside of the body. This evidence will help them find out the name of the person, the time of their death, and if a crime has been committed.

Bugs and Time

Bugs can help determine time of death. Certain bugs are attracted to old, dry bodies. Others are drawn to fresher bodies. Blowflies can smell a body within fifteen minutes of death and lay their eggs on the body. Maggots then hatch from the eggs and eat the body. The maggots eventually grow into blowflies. Scientists study the age of the bugs on the body and then they count backward to determine when the person died.

Close-up of a blowfly

Wounds and Weapons

Wounds and bruising can help determine if a person fell or if they were struck. They can also show what kind of weapon was used based on the person's injuries. Forensic scientists compare the shape of an injury with the shape of a knife, or the grooves of bullets with the ridges inside of a gun.

Bone Evidence

What if there is no body and only bones are found? A skeleton can tell a lot about a person. By studying the skeleton of the body, scientists can find the age, gender, possible injuries, or

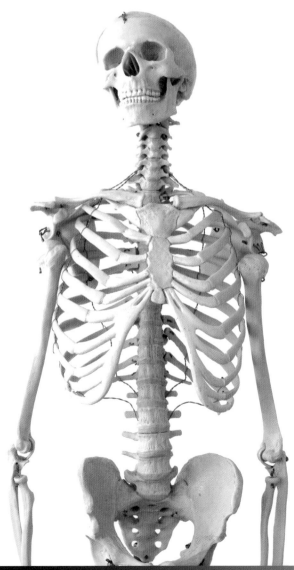

Skeletons can give many clues about someone.

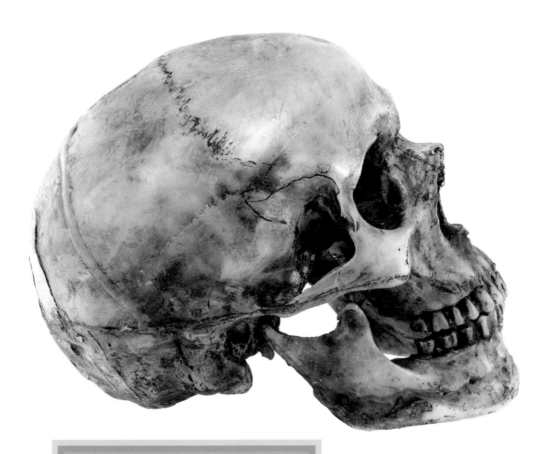

Scientists can find evidence
of injuries in skulls.

diseases the person may have had. Skeletons can even
reveal information about diet, lifestyle, ancestry, and
cause of death.

Skulls can be reconstructed, meaning they can be
rebuilt. By looking at the bone structure, facial recognition
technology can compare the structure of the skull to
images of people and help find a missing person.

A 3D printed section of bone attached to a model skull

With 3D technology, forensic scientists can make digital copies of fragile bones. Exact copies of pieces of bones can be made and put together like a puzzle. When bones don't have to be handled, the evidence is less likely to break.

STEM Spotlight

Scientists reconstruct a face by making a mold of the skull, including the jaw and eye sockets. They use depth markers of different lengths and attach them to the skull. The length of each marker is determined by how thick a person's facial tissue would be based on their age, gender, and race. Scientists make a cast to add depth to the mold. Then they add facial muscles. They finish building the face with clay and make mathematical guesses to build the eyes, nose, and mouth.

Chapter 3

SOLVING CASES

The smallest sample of DNA can bring big results. DNA stands for deoxyribonucleic acid. It contains genetic information that makes each person unique. It is found in almost every cell of the body. This includes cells in the skin, muscle, hair, bones, and blood.

Looking at DNA

Scientists can analyze a person's bodily fluids to find out their gender, age, or if they have taken any drugs. DNA analysis can give police predictions of a person's traits such as hair, eye, and skin color.

Teeth store DNA. Since teeth are inside of the mouth, they are more protected than other parts of the body. Teeth are hard, so they do not decay as fast and don't usually get destroyed in disasters like a fire. Forensic scientists can analyze teeth to identify a person.

A person looking at DNA

Looking at a Scene

Forensic scientists study the surroundings of a crime. They take samples of things from the scene such as a shoe print or speck of dirt. Then they can test the samples in a lab and see if either of them match something found on a suspect. If they match, the suspect may be guilty.

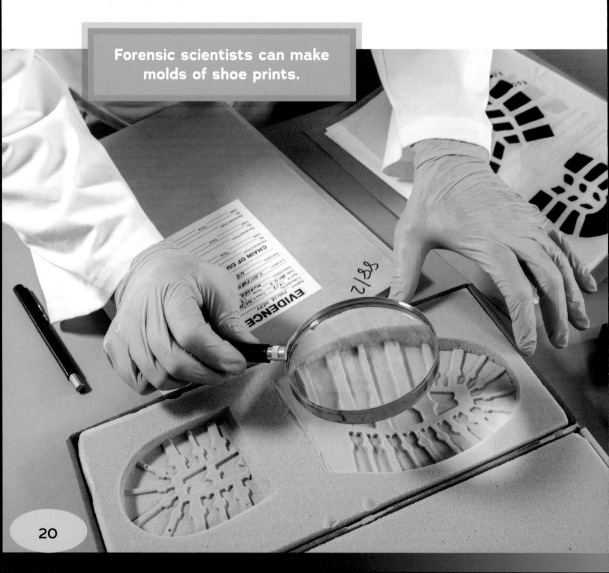

Forensic scientists can make molds of shoe prints.

With the use of alternative light photography, forensic scientists can see things that can't be seen by the naked eye. The scientists attach certain filters to ultraviolet lights and can find evidence like saliva and blood, fingerprints and footprint impressions, and hidden messages using special inks. This special lighting can even show damage to a person underneath their skin before a bruise appears.

Digital evidence is information stored on electronic devices or online.

Digital Traces

A lot can be found out about a person by studying their habits in the digital world. Many people leave information on their phones, laptops, video games, and social media platforms that show where they have been and what they have been doing.

Some cars have technology that shows how an accident or crash occurred. They also store information on places drivers have been, including their regular routes and favorite locations.

Chapter 4

THE FORENSIC FUTURE

The digital world continues to advance. Advances in technology are helping forensic scientists when they are investigating a crime.

LOOKING AT EVIDENCE FROM DRONES IS CALLED DRONE FORENSICS.

New Technology

The public, scientists, and the military use drones. But sometimes people use drones for illegal activity. Drone forensics studies these activities. Scientists gather evidence from drones like video footage and location data. Scientists can also track down the owner of a drone. As drone activity increases, drone forensics will advance and be used more.

Handheld forensic devices are available and will become more common for on-site testing and results. These devices are useful to investigators searching for drugs or other toxins that a person may have taken. The test results come through quickly on site without having to wait for a lab to process the sample.

Forensic scientists bring many tools to a crime scene, such as the materials needed to make a cast of a footprint.

Science Fact or Science Fiction?

We have learned all we can from fingerprint analysis.

That is fiction! For over one hundred years, fingerprint analysis has been used in investigations. Through research, scientists are learning that some materials of a fingerprint decay faster than others. In the future, investigators will know when a fingerprint was placed at a scene, which will assist in the timeline of an event and location of a suspect.

A scientist studying proteins

New Testing

Biology advances forensics. Forensic science is going deeper into the study of proteins in bones, blood, and other biological materials. Tests only need a small sample of protein. Scientists analyze the sample and work backward to find the DNA code that made the protein. They can learn the DNA of the sample without having the DNA evidence.

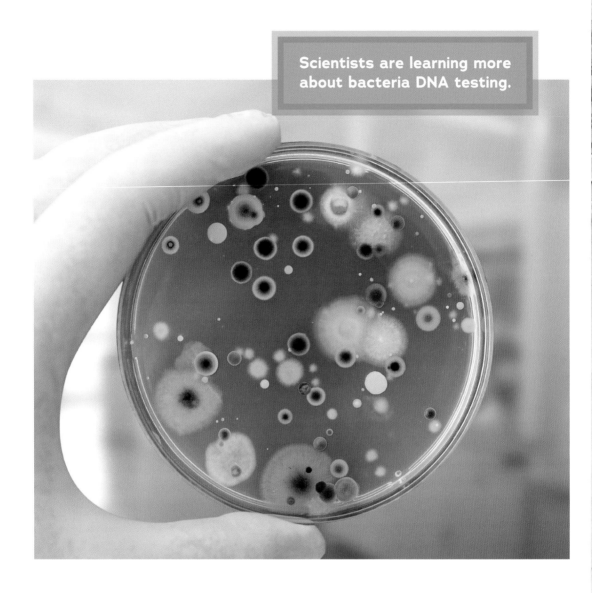

Scientists are learning more about bacteria DNA testing.

There are trillions of microorganisms of bacteria in our bodies. Bacteria lives in places like our skin, gums, teeth, and even in our breath. DNA testing may enable scientists to analyze bacteria left behind by a suspect's breath to find out who they are!

Forensic scientists continue to work hard to stay ahead of crime. Further research in all areas of science will improve their ability to assist in investigations and to examine physical evidence.

A forensic scientist photographing a crime scene

Glossary

analyze: to examine and explain

autopsy: an examination of a dead body to figure out the cause of death

decompose: to rot

evidence: something that shows proof

forensic science: the use of scientific knowledge to solve a crime

genetic information: information about a person's genes, which determines characteristics such as eye color

microorganism: a microscopic organism, especially a bacterium, virus, or fungus

protein: a molecule in the body that helps regulate tissues and organs

reconstruct: to build again

toxin: a poisonous substance

trace evidence: evidence created when objects make contact

Learn More

Explain That Stuff! Forensic Science
https://www.explainthatstuff.com/forensicscience.html

Forensic Science Facts
https://www.sciencekids.co.nz/sciencefacts/forensicscience.html

Messner, Kate, and Ruppert, Anne. *Solve This: Forensics*. Washington, DC: National Geographic, 2020.

PBS LearningMedia: Crime Scene Investigation
https://illinois.pbslearningmedia.org/resource/idptv11.sci.life.gen
.d4kcsi/crime-scene-investigation/

Ross, Melissa. *Forensics for Kids: The Science and History of Crime Solving, with 21 Activities*. Chicago: Chicago Review Press, 2022.

Starr, Abbe Lynn. *Explore Nanotechnology*. Minneapolis: Lerner Publications, 2024.

Index

Photo Acknowledgments

Images used: Keystone/Hulton Archive/Getty Images, p. 5; Musa_Studio/Shutterstock, p .6; Tonhom1009/Shutterstock, p. 7; Coast-to-Coast/Getty Images, p. 8; PRESSLAB/Shutterstock, p. 9; LightFieldStudios/Getty Images, p. 11; Vladimir Borovic/Shutterstock, p. 12; Winai Pantho/Shutterstock, p. 13; Arcady/Shutterstock, p. 14; witoon214/Shutterstock, p. 15; Bloomberg/Getty Images, p. 16; MICHAEL DONNE, UNIVERSITY OF MANCHESTER/Science Source, p. 17; Peter Dazeley/Getty Images, p. 19; felipe caparros/Shutterstock, p. 20; fired1991/Getty Images, p. 21; Endorphin_SK/Shutterstock, p. 22; Kypros/Getty Images, p. 24; DarSzach/Shutterstock, p. 25; Cultura RM Exclusive/Sigrid Gombert/Getty Images, p. 27; Kateryna Kon/Shutterstock, p. 28; Stocked House Studio/Shutterstock, p. 29.

Cover: Andrew Brookes/Getty Images.